Unmanned Aerial Vehicle Operations

I0439931

U.S. Marine Corps

PCN 143 000141 00

To Our Readers

Changes: Readers of this publication are encouraged to submit suggestions and changes that will improve it. Recommendations may be sent directly to Commanding General, Marine Corps Combat Development Command, Doctrine Division (C 42), 3300 Russell Road, Suite 318A, Quantico, VA 22134-5021 or by fax to 703-784-2917 (DSN 278-2917) or by E-mail to **morgann@mccdc.usmc.mil**. Recommendations should include the following information:

- Location of change
  Publication number and title
  Current page number
  Paragraph number (if applicable)
  Line number
  Figure or table number (if applicable)
- Nature of change
  Add, delete
  Proposed new text, preferably double-
  spaced and typewritten
- Justification and/or source of change

Additional copies: A printed copy of this publication may be obtained from Marine Corps Logistics Base, Albany, GA 31704-5001, by following the instructions in MCBul 5600, *Marine Corps Doctrinal Publications Status*. An electronic copy may be obtained from the Doctrine Division, MCCDC, world wide web home page which is found at the following universal reference locator: **http://www.doctrine.usmc.mil**.

DEPARTMENT OF THE NAVY
Headquarters United States Marine Corps
Washington, DC 20380-1775

14 August 2003

FOREWORD

Marine Corps Warfighting Publication (MCWP) 3-42.1, *Unmanned Aerial Vehicle Operations*, addresses the fundamentals of planning and execution of unmanned aerial vehicle (UAV) operations in support of the Marine air-ground task force (MAGTF).

A UAV is a powered, aerial vehicle that does not carry a human operator, uses aerodynamic forces to provide vehicle lift, can fly autonomously or be piloted remotely, can be expendable or recoverable, and can carry a lethal or nonlethal payload. Ballistic or semiballistic vehicles, cruise missiles, and artillery projectiles are not considered UAVs.

This publication provides guidance to commanders, their staffs, and UAV squadron personnel. It addresses planning requirements, command and support relationships, request procedures, and UAV capabilities.

MCWP 3-42.1 supersedes Fleet Marine Force Manual (FMFM) 3-22-1, *UAV Company Operations,* dated 4 November 1993.

Reviewed and approved this date.

BY DIRECTION OF THE COMMANDANT OF THE MARINE CORPS

EDWARD HANLON, JR.
Lieutenant General, U.S. Marine Corps
Commanding General
Marine Corps Combat Development Command

Publication Control Number: 143 000141 00

Unmanned Aerial Vehicle Operations

Table of Contents

Chapter 3. Planning

Chapter 4. Execution

Appendixes

Chapter 1
Fundamentals

Marine Unmanned Aerial Vehicle Squadron

The Marine unmanned aerial vehicle squadron (VMU) provides personnel to support, maintain, and operate unmanned aerial vehicle (UAV) systems. Its mission is to operate and maintain a UAV system to provide unmanned aerial reconnaissance support to the Marine Expeditionary Force (MEF) or other supported units. The VMU performs the following tasks:

- Conduct aerial reconnaissance, surveillance, and target acquisition (RSTA) operations.

- Perform airborne surveillance of designated target areas, Marine air-ground task force (MAGTF) areas of interest/influence, and other areas as directed.

- Perform airborne surveillance for search and rescue and for tactical recovery of aircraft and personnel.

- Perform reconnaissance of helicopter approach and retirement lanes in support of vertical assaults.

- Provide real-time target information to the direct air support center (DASC) and fire support coordination center (FSCC) to adjust fire missions and close air support.

- Provide information to assist adjusting indirect fire weapons and support deep air support and air interdiction.

- Collect battle damage assessment (BDA)/bomb hit assessment.

- Support rear area security.

- Provide a remote-receive station capability and liaison to des-ignated units.

- Conduct individual and unit training to prepare for tactical employment and combat operations.

The VMU is comprised of the following:

- Administrative department.

- Intelligence department.

- Logistics and supply department.

- Safety department with Naval Air Training and Operating Procedures Standardization (NATOPS), aviation safety, and ground safety sections.

- Operations department. The operations department maintains ground training, aviation training, the UAV pilot's NATOPS flight records, and current and future operations section.

- Aviation maintenance department. The aviation maintenance department maintains the UAV and its ground equipment as prescribed by appropriate aviation maintenance publications and technical manuals associated with the UAV system.

- Communications platoon. A communications platoon may be attached or assigned to the VMU to support UAV operations in garrison or in the field. For effective communication within the command, control, communications, computers, intelligence, surveillance, and reconnaissance architecture, radiomen, wire-men, and computer technicians (with their equipment) must be used during each mission.

- Motor transportation section. The motor transportation section may be attached. It operates and maintains the rolling stock to transport squadron personnel and the UAV system.

The Threat

The threat to UAVs is similar to that of other low performance aircraft. See *Unmanned Aerial Vehicle Survivability Threat Assessment Report, Short Range Pioneer Remotely Piloted Vehicle System Survivability and Vulnerability,* and *Pacific Missile Test Center and Joint System Threat Assessment Report, Close Range Unmanned Aerial Vehicle (CR-UAV) (S),* for detailed threat descriptions.

Because the initial UAV systems are designed primarily for low to mid-intensity conflict, many integrated air defense systems (IADSs) can be used against UAV operations. The major threat is from antiaircraft artillery (AAA) and man portable air defense systems.

UAV operations are vulnerable to enemy electronic warfare (EW). Enemy EW would be directed at the systems controlling the UAV, the UAV, and the information downlinks that provide real-time combat information. The enemy could employ ground-based and airborne (helicopter or fixed-wing) electronic attack (EA).

A threat exists from enemy rotary- and fixed-wing aircraft. Attack helicopters have a limited air-to-air intercept capability, which poses a significant threat to UAVs.

The Role of Unmanned Aerial Vehicles

During military operations other than war, a UAV provides the MAGTF with useful information about the area of operations and forewarns of any emerging threats in the vicinity by loitering overhead and providing real-time intelligence.

UAVs play a valuable role in amphibious operations. UAV intelligence information links to ships and provides real-time intelligence to the combat operations center (COC) and planning cells onboard. During execution, the UAV provides support in operations against enemy forces, obstructions, IADS, deep strike targets, and landing zones. It can observe and adjust naval gunfire in the amphibious objective area (AOA).

UAVs in special operations require connectivity with personnel that have access to the information provided by the UAV. UAVs can fly over the objective area days, hours or minutes ahead of special operations forces and provide valuable intelligence.

Emerging Concepts

Technological advances will continue to provide unprecedented leaps in UAV capability. The Navy and Marine Corps are primarily concerned with UAV technology as it applies to the Expeditionary Maneuver Warfare (EMW) concept. The Marine Corps will continue to focus its effort towards amphibious operations and all other missions and tasks in or around littoral areas. The high tempo of operations essential to successful operational maneuver from the sea requires that intelligence be provided to decisionmakers with a minimum of delay. Technology that permits the rapid dissemination of intelligence products will play an important role in this effort.

The Marine Corps desires an organic UAV that is interoperable with joint command, control, communications, and computers systems, can operate from ships/seabases, and will seamlessly transition to operations ashore. This future UAV system should have the capability to support EMW, and therefore, must be deployable by organic Marine Corps aviation assets. UAV systems should be organized to provide scalable support to Marine Expeditionary Units (MEUs), Marine Expeditionary Brigades, and MEFs. Most importantly, the UAV system must be responsive to the needs of the MAGTF commander by providing reconnaissance, target designation, communications/data relay, and signals intelligence (SIGINT) capabilities through the use of modular payloads. Ideally, the UAV should be able to launch from a ship, provide persistent support to the MAGTF commander during movement to the objective (as well as during actions on the objective), while being able to return to the ship/seabase or land at a pre-designated site ashore. The future UAV system must be very reliable with low mean time between failures and low maintenance manhours per flight hour. The UAV must be maintainable in austere environments while requiring minimal manpower for servicing.

Chapter 2
Command, Control, and Communications

Command

The VMU is organic to the Marine aircraft wing and is under the command of the aviation combat element (ACE). The ACE commander exercises command, control, and communications via the ACE G-3/S-3 and the Marine air command and control system (MACCS).

Command Relationships

Marine units may be either organic or attached. The VMU is organic to the ACE and follows the ACE's administrative and operational chain of command. Attachment of the squadron or provision of detachments to MAGTFs smaller than a MEF are also possible. When attached, planners must consider unique UAV logistics and operational support requirements.

Support Relationships

Support relationships are mission assignments in which one commander supports another. Unlike command relationships, support relationships specify only the priority of effort of the supporting unit. They do not transfer responsibility for or control beyond the authority to specify priority of tasks to the supported commander. Allocation of UAV support must reflect a balanced decision on how to best exploit UAV capabilities. The VMU or elements of the squadron are employed in general support (GS) or direct support (DS).

General Support

When the UAV squadron or a detachment operates in GS, it supports the entire MAGTF. The MAGTF commander determines priority of support and resolves any conflicts. Priority of support to subordinate elements will likely go to the unit that is the main effort. GS better enables the ACE commander to provide UAV capabilities to the force as a whole, as well as to respond to requirements of higher and adjacent headquarters. When the MAGTF commander employs the VMU in GS, it is critical that he ensures that all MAGTF elements have the best possible access to UAV support.

Direct Support

When the VMU operates in DS, it responds to a specific, designated unit, supporting the supported unit's specific stated requirements. Priority of support goes to the supported unit but other missions may be performed provided they do not interfere with completion of the supported unit requirements. Under DS, the VMU or detachment should provide liaison to the supported unit to coordinate requirements and mission tasking. Due to the limited communication assets held by the VMU, the means of communication between the UAV unit and the supported unit need to be identified early in the planning process. These lines of communications will be necessary for efficient coordination of support and dissemination of information. UAVs providing DS afford the best and most timely response to the major subordinate command (MSC) commander to whom control has been delegated. The supported commander can specify the time and place for intelligence collection missions and can receive near real-time information during missions.

Control

Control is the means through which the commander extends his authority. The MAGTF commander exercises control by establishing both command and support relationships based on informational requirements within the force. Command relationships define how the force is to be organized. Support relationships define who is to be supported and who is to provide that support. Support relationships are established by the commander to weigh his main effort by prioritizing support within the force.

Aviation Command, Control, and Communications Systems

Because UAVs are aircraft, other forms of control specific to aviation apply to their employment. The most common are air control, airspace control, and air direction, which are exercised by MACCS personnel and agencies.

Navy Tactical Air Control Center

The Navy tactical air control center (Navy TACC) will normally be established as the control agency responsible for all air operations within the AOA. The amphibious task force commander is responsible for the organization and employment of the Navy TACC.

Marine Air Command and Control System

The MACCS provides the MAGTF commander with the capabilities to command, control, coordinate, and manage the ACE supporting the MAGTF. Similar to the Navy TACC, the MACCS provides for centralized command, coordination, and supervision of air operations at the highest level while incorporating decentralized control to subordinate agencies. The MACCS is task-organized to provide personnel and equipment to authority over and direction of all air operations. The MACCS is tasked with the control and coordination of offensive air support, assault support, air reconnaissance, antiair warfare, and EW functions of Marine aviation. The MACCS is also responsible for the control and coordination of the MAGTF's IADS within the MAGTF's area of operations.

Air Control

Air control is the authority to direct the physical maneuver of a UAV in flight or direct a UAV to image a specific target. MCWP 3-25, *Control of Aircraft and Missiles*, defines control of aircraft and missiles as "the coordinated employment of facilities, equipment, communications, procedures, and personnel that allows the ACE commander to plan, direct, and control the efforts of the ACE to support the accomplishment of the MAGTF's mission."

Airspace Control

Airspace control is a form of air control. Airspace control provides for the coordination, integration, regulation of the use of a defined airspace, and identification of all airspace users. Any airborne object that may interfere with the flight path or trajectory of any other object within the MAGTF's airspace is of concern and has some influence on the control of aircraft and missiles. Aircraft, including UAVs, friendly supporting arms fire, and surface-to-air weapons are airspace users. Their employment requires airspace coordination and integration.

Airspace control is the authority to direct the maneuver of a UAV (along with other aircraft and airspace users) for the best use of the airspace. Airspace control is accomplished through established procedures for coordination of air, artillery, naval surface fire support, and UAV plans by appropriate MAGTF elements. Principles and procedures of airspace control used in manned flight operations apply to UAV operations. UAVs are normally routed through existing air control points by airspace control agencies. Airspace control authority is inherent in the commander whose unit is responsible for particular blocks of airspace, types of missions or types of aircraft. It does not include measures to approve, disapprove, deny or delay UAV operations.

Positive separation between aircraft and UAVs is required and is the responsibility of the appropriate airspace control agency. This may be accomplished by the following:

- Activating temporary airspace coordination areas (ACAs); Class D airspace or restricted operations zones (ROZs) for UAV takeoffs and landings; and mission areas or flight routes. ROZs are also known as restricted operations areas (ROAs).

- Routing separation via existing air control points. Specific UAV routes may be created by connecting selected air control points together.

- Altitude separation that can be effected by having block altitudes or by deconflicting whatever altitude the UAV is flying with other airspace users.

- Time separation that can be effected by having block times for UAV operations.

- Any combination of the above can be used, as required.

- Dynamic/real-time integration of the UAV into the airspace is achieved through coordination between the supporting arms coordination center/Navy TACC afloat or the FSCC and DASC ashore.

Air Direction

The purpose of air direction is to achieve a balance between the use of the MAGTF's finite UAV assets and the ability of the VMU to accomplish its mission. Inefficient air direction results in poor use of resources and excessive response times. Air direction is exercised by the ACE commander through the MACCS. Air direction tasks include but are not limited to the following:

- Develop UAV missions for inclusion into the air tasking order (ATO).

- Fulfill ATO requirements.

- Dynamic re-tasking of a UAV's mission.

- Process requests for UAV support.

- Collect information on UAV mission status.

- Move UAV units to new operating sites.

- Adjust VMU mission assignments within previously set parameters due to air or ground tactical situation changes.

Communications

Existing doctrinal communications nets connect the VMU with supported units and airspace management agencies (see MCWP 3-40.3). These nets are established to satisfy communications requirements during amphibious operations and subsequent operations ashore. They are not intended to preclude establishing circuits to meet unique requirements. The UAV mission commander is required to maintain two-way communications with the airspace management agency throughout flight operations. Additional coordination nets may be established between supported units.

Radio Links and Nets

UAV Primary Up Link Control	Transmits commands that control the UAV and payload during flight operations.
UAV Secondary Up Link Control	Provides signals to control the UAV and payload during flight operations if the UAV primary up link control becomes inoperative.
TAD (UHF/VHF) or the TACT (UHF/VHF) Net	Used by the mission commander or UAV operator to coordinate airspace during flight operations. Radios in the control station provide simultaneous monitoring of one of these nets and the international guard frequency. Positive communications between the DASC (or an appropriate air control agency) and the mission commander is required for all UAV flight operations.
UAV Telemetry Down Link	Provides real-time video display of the target area from the UAV. It also provides display of down link flight control data to the control station.
UAV Command Net (VHF/UHF)	Used by the UAV mission commander to coordinate UAV activities on the airfield. If the launch and recovery site is located at an extended distance from a control station, it may be necessary to establish this net via HF radio. Whenever possible a telephone wire system should be installed as the primary communications means between the mission commander and other mission-essential activities.
LF INTEL (HF/VHF/UHF-SATCOM) Net	Provides a current situational information exchange with the MAGTF SARC. This net is used by the UAV mission commander and the SARC. Whenever possible, wire is the primary communication means among these stations.
Air Spot Net	Used for fire missions.

Voice Nets	The VMU can enter any of the doctrinal voice radio nets identified in MCWP 3-40.3. When distance or time prevents establishing a telephone network, the following radio nets may be established from existing T/E assets.
HD (UHF/VHF) Net	Used by the mission commander for close coordination between the UAV mission commander and helicopters.
NGF Spot (HF) Net	Used by the mission commander to assist the NSFS ship adjust fire support and provide target damage assessment.
FSC (HF/UHF) Net	This net is used by the mission commander to coordinate or adjust supporting arms fire through the supported FSCC or artillery unit headquarters.
COF (HF/UHF) Net	This net is used by the mission commander when adjusting artillery missions directly with the artillery battery or battalion.
LF RECON (HF/VHF/UHF-SATCOM) Net	Provides for coordination of the reconnaissance effort within the MAGTF. This net is between the mission commander and the reconnaissance unit. It is an alternate communication means to pass critical information from the reconnaissance unit when the doctrinal intelligence net is unavailable.
LF TAC or GCE TAC (HF/UHF) Net	Issued to pass FLASH precedence traffic when other means are not available. It may also aid the GCE commander in maneuver control

LEGEND

COF = conduct of fire
FSC = fire support coordination
GCE = ground combat element (MAGTF)
HD = helicopter direction
HF = high frequency
LF INTEL = landing force intelligence
LF RECON = landing force
   reconnaissance
NGF = naval gunfire
NSFS = naval surface fire support

SARC= surveillance and reconnaissance center
SATCOM = satellite communications
TAC = tactical
TACT = tactical aviation control team
TAD = tactical air direction
T/E= table of equipment
UHF = ultra high frequency
VHF = very high frequency

Frequency Separation

Frequency allocation and control, especially UAV up link and down link control frequencies, must be carefully coordinated with the MAGTF G-6/S-6 to reduce adjacent channel interference and enhance flight safety. The MAGTF electronic warfare officer (EWO) excludes the UAV up link and down link control frequencies from any friendly induced interference.

Communications Security

Communications security is a principal consideration in all communications planning due to UAV vulnerability to enemy jamming.

Chapter 3
Planning

Deployment within the Continental United States

Before any military deployment, considerable planning takes place well in advance of the operation. Uavs increase the workload on personnel assigned this task who very often know little about the unique requirements of UAV integration in exercises in the continental United States (CONUS) or overseas. The ACE commander must decide early if the UAV will be employed so coordination with appropriate agencies or countries can occur.

Certificate of Authorization

The Federal Aviation Administration (FAA) is responsible for airspace management within the US. If a UAV will be flown outside the boundaries of special use airspace, sufficient time must be allowed to authorize UAV operations.

A request must be submitted to the regional FAA where the operation will be conducted in accordance with FAA regulations (see appendix A). Specific details about dates, times, areas or routes, altitudes, and a description of the UAV are included in this request.

The regional FAA administrator will draft a certificate of authorization, which sets forth the requirements for UAV personnel qualifications, communications procedures, and a definition of the requested airspace. Other items are included as the regional FAA administrator determines.

A UAV cannot fly beyond the boundaries of special use airspace without the specific authorization of the FAA and the local air traffic control authority.

Memorandum of Understanding

A memorandum of understanding with the local air traffic control facility is required to ensure they and the ACE commander have a complete understanding and agree to the air traffic control procedures that will be used to ensure safe UAV operations in the operating area. If additional air traffic control services are required, the ACE commander may be asked to augment the local air traffic control facility with additional air traffic control personnel.

Letter of Agreement

A letter of agreement with local air facilities is required to ensure proper coordination of support requirements are understood and agreed to. Fuel and hazardous material storage, hanger facilities, runway use or any other logistical and support requirements should be agreed on in this document.

Deployment Overseas

UAVs are a relatively inexpensive intelligence-gathering tool. The rapid growth of these systems will continue to increase as technology advances and economies of scale provide affordable platforms and equipment. Foreign governments are sensitive to the valuable information and capabilities of UAV systems as well as the inherent risks associated with unmanned flight operations. ACE planners must ensure UAV operations are included at the outset of integration planning within host nation (HN) airspace. Planners should have a firm understanding of the of the UAV system to be employed to positively satisfy any protest or concerns from the HN. The US Embassy or consulate in the HN must be notified of UAV operations within their represented country.

Waivers, agreements, and rules by the International Civil Aviation Organization, the HN's government, the US Embassy, and the ACE commander must be thoroughly understood and signed before conducting UAV operations overseas.

Transportation Requirements

Transportation requirements for a UAV system will vary from system to system and the size of the UAV unit being deployed. The MAGTF G-4 must become familiar with the unique transportation requirements of whatever UAV system will be deployed.

Pioneer UAV items are helicopter-transportable with some disassembly required. The current UAV unit T/E provides sufficient organic motor transport to move the entire unit over road and across country. UAV systems are routinely transported across the US by rail and truck. Overseas deployment can be accomplished by airlift or sealift. Airlift provides for quick deployment to regional areas, but can require considerable lift support. Sealift is used primarily for MEU deployments.

Supply Support

The ACE provides supply support. The objective of supply support is to establish, maintain, and improve combat readiness by ensuring that supply support is available for the UAV system when it becomes operational. In the appropriate echelons of the supply and maintenance system, supply support makes available all spares and repair parts, support and test equipment, and technical assistance to support the UAV system when it becomes operational. It also ensures that additional stocks are available through routine replenishment.

Supply support includes acquisition, distribution, provisioning, inventory replenishment of system components, spares, repair parts, and consumable supplies needed to maintain the system in a high state of readiness. Supply support for non-UAV systems is provided in accordance with existing Marine Corps policies for provisioning and supplies. The Marine Corps logistics base and the supported commander share supply responsibility. Initial spares support is provided by contract for short-range UAV system-unique items. Classes of supply requiring special considerations follow.

Class III, Fuel

Besides standard petroleum, oils, and lubricants (POL) requirements for T/E items, the Pioneer UAV requires 100-octane motor gasoline and engine oil. Future UAV systems may require jet fuel, such as JP-5, and oil suitable for turbine engine operations.

Class V, Ordnance

If rocket assisted takeoff (RATO) launch is planned, provision for the storage, transportation, and use of rocket assemblies must be made. If ordnance-induced, activation devices can deploy emergency systems, such as parachutes. Provision must be made for use of these devices.

Class IX, Repair Parts

Under current arrangements for the Pioneer UAV, the contractor is contractually obligated to provide operational spares, 30-day pack-up kits for extended training, and 90-day pack-up kits for deployment. Stockage for the UAV system will not be loaded into the inventory system. In an operational situation, the ACE will also provide for the evacuation of parts, that are beyond the capability to repair at the unit level. Commanders may have to provide transportation of evacuated materials to CONUS. Once items reach CONUS, the contractor will provide transportation to the depot maintenance facility.

See appendix B for Pioneer UAV system characteristics.

Engineer Support

When a suitable site for the conduct of UAV operations cannot be located, engineer support may be required for site preparation; for example, Pioneer requires an area 75 feet by 2,000 feet. If paved runways, improved roads (asphalt or concrete), and unimproved roads (hard dirt) are available, then they can be used for takeoff and landing operations. In this case, engineering support will not be required.

Firepower

The VMU has organic small arms for self-defense. It requires security forces from the supported unit if the tactical situation calls for a defensive posture.

Medical

The VMU has a corpsman for minor injuries and emergency treatment. It relies on the ACE commander or the supported unit for further medical support.

Messing

The VMU does not have a messing capability. The supported unit, Marine wing support squadron or ACE provides support.

Operations Site

Particular consideration must be given to the location of the UAV operations site. Depending on the UAV system, an adequate runway may be required for safe UAV operations. At a minimum, a proper landing surface must be available to safely recover the UAV upon completing its mission.

Consideration must also be given to the distance from the UAV operations site to the area of operations (AO). Many UAVs are not particularly fast and require considerable time to fly to their mission area. The location of an adequate launch and recovery area and its distance to the AO and control station are very important considerations when employing a UAV system.

Availability of adequate roads or other transportation methods for resupply of fuel and other UAV support requirements are critical to sustained UAV operations. If the UAV system is expected to move from one site to another, transportation support becomes increasingly important.

Weather

The ACE collections and operations officers must consider the expected weather conditions in the AO at the time of operations. Many UAVs cannot operate in inclement weather; for example, high winds and precipitation or when the cloud layer is below the UAV's operating altitude. Due consideration must be given to probable weather conditions from the outset.

Communication

To provide the MAGTF commander with adequate support, the UAV system should be linked to the command and control architecture of the MACCS.

Control Frequencies

Each UAV system has unique control frequency ranges. The VMU must ensure that its control frequencies are adequately separated from other communications frequencies. The VMU must continue to be aware of EW frequencies as operations progress to eliminate the possibility of interference from other assets while airborne.

Bandwidth

Adequate bandwidth is required to supply real-time or near real-time UAV intelligence information. The ACE G-2/S-2 must determine what the UAV is expected to provide and ensure communications support is provided to the VMU.

Operation Phases

UAV operations are conducted similarly to manned aviation operations. Once the VMU commander receives the ATO with the mission, many tasks are executed simultaneously.

Responsibilities

Through the ATO, the ACE commander assigns the VMU commander with a mission. The current operations section then begins the planning process. Together with the intelligence section, the UAV flight crew studies the assigned mission and plans for its execution. The maintenance crew begins preparation of the UAV and the UAV ground system, while communications personnel ensure that the proper communication connectivity is provided to fulfill the mission.

Route Planning

UAV missions will be planned by the VMU in close coordination with the ACE collections, future plans, and future operations. This is done to ensure deconfliction with other ACE operations and to allow timely inclusion of UAV missions into the ATO planning process. See figure 3-1 on page 3-10 for a UAV planning matrix.

Deceptive Routes

UAV routing can deceive and expose the enemy. The enemy may notice a UAV flying in a certain direction to a certain location, and conclude the UAV is on a route reconnaissance mission. The enemy may then relocate resources to defend a perceived attack.

Airspace managers must guard against using the same route of flight for missions to similar locations. When the enemy becomes familiar with the flight pattern of the UAV, the airborne platform becomes a more easily processed target for enemy IADS.

When planning a UAV route, as with any airborne asset, attention must be given to enemy IADS. Unless the mission is to expose possible air defense sites, the UAV should be routed around possible enemy air defenses to increase the UAV's ability to complete its mission.

Target Considerations
  Target Description
  Target Coordinates
    Latitude/Longitude
    Grid
	Area of Operations
	  Latitude/Longitude
	  Grid

Launch and Recovery Area
  Latitude/Longitude
  Grid
  Outbound Heading
  Outbound Altitude
	Waypoints and Checkpoints
	  Latitude/Longitude
	  Assigned Altitude
	  Outbound Heading

Special Airspace
  Corridors
    Entry Point Latitude/Longitude
    Entry Point Grid
    Entry Altitude
    Transit Heading(s)
    Transit Altitude
    Exit Altitude
    Exit Point Latitude/Longitude
    Exit Point Grid
	Holding Area
	  Latitude/Longitude
	  Grid
	  Altitude

Return Home Point
  Latitude/Longitude
  Grid
  Enroute Altitude
  Action Upon Arrival
    Orbit Altitude
    Ditch
	Payload Type

Distance: Control Station to Target	Administrative Considerations Are standing operating procedures (SOPs), LOAs, and MOUs current?

Frequency Considerations
  UAV Control Link
    Uplink
    Downlink
    Separation from Other Agencies
      Uplink: _____MHz
      Downlink: _____MHz
	Communications Considerations
	  Controlling Agency
	    UHF:
	    VHF:
	  Supported Unit
	    UHF
	    VHF
	    HF

Maps
  Are up-to-date maps available?
	Execution
	  Brief Time
	  Launch Time
	  Time Over Target
	  Recovery Time
	  Total Mission Time
	  Debrief Time

Figure 3-1. Unmanned Aerial Vehicle Planning Matrix.

In-flight Emergencies

During planning, sufficient attention must be given to the possibility that an in-flight emergency may occur. Particular attention should be given to the location of friendly ground forces if the UAV exits controlled flight and impacts the ground. Flight paths, minimum-risk routes, and other air management tools must be included.

Loss of Link Procedures

When the UAV senses a significant delay or loss of the command up link, it will automatically enter into a return home mode of flight. The return home profile will be determined before launch by the UAV pilot. When the UAV pilot recognizes the UAV is on its return home profile, emergency procedures will be performed as required in the UAV NATOPS manual.

The UAV will fly a pre-approved route at a pre-approved altitude to its pre-approved return home site. At the return home site, the UAV will perform the program flight maneuver unless commanded otherwise by the UAV pilot.

During this emergency, the UAV pilot will attempt to reestablish communication with the UAV. If contact is reestablished, the mission commander may choose to terminate the mission and return to base or continue with the mission as planned.

Agency Notification

Upon notification of an in-flight emergency, the mission commander will ensure emergency procedures are being performed by UAV pilots in accordance with the UAV NATOPS manual.

The mission commander will notify the appropriate air control agency to coordinate changes to the route of flight.

The mission commander will notify the DASC and inform the senior watch officer (SWO) of the emergency and the UAV's expected route of flight. The DASC will then relay and coordinate with the appropriate agencies; for example, TACC or FSCC.

The SWO will ensure that air control agencies have been notified of the UAV emergency and its expected course. Controlling agencies will ensure that other air assets are separated from the UAV's expected route of flight and notify the SWO of any further actions taken.

Friendly air defense assets and ground forces should be notified if the SWO deems the information useful for the safety of personnel on the ground.

Chapter 4
Execution

Collection Tasking

If the VMU must provide for its own security when deployed, the ability to support sustained operations for a long duration will be reduced. The conduct of a UAV flight will differ somewhat depending on the UAV system. However, there are basic phases common to each system.

UAVs are employed in many intelligence, surveillance, and reconnaissance and target acquisition roles, supporting a variety of units. The variety of possible missions and supported units requires integration and coordination in planning and execution. It also requires a means to assign missions, task UAVs, and exercise authority over UAV operations. Collection tasking authority is the authority to task the VMU commander to collect information that will be used as combat information or to develop intelligence. Collection tasking authority resides with the commander who has control of the VMU.

Organic Assets

Preplanned and immediate UAV requests are submitted to the controlling headquarters using DD Form 1972, *Joint Tactical Air Strike Request (JTAR)*, to identify targets, locations, times, and coordinating instructions in as much detail as possible. (See appendix C.)

Preplanned

Preplanned UAV missions are initiated when the MAGTF receives requests for UAV support via the JTAR. A JTAR for UAV support goes through the same process as a rotary- or fixed-wing request. Based on the MAGTF commander's concept of operations and the commander's critical information requirements, the MEF G-2 will task the ACE with aerial reconnaissance requirements. If the ACE cannot satisfy these requirements with existing assets, this will be made known to the collection officer. Unsatisfied requirements may be adjudicated through a collection integration and synchronization board (CISB) or similar coordination board. For smaller MAGTFs, the CISB process will still occur in the form of a meeting between the MAGTF S-2/S-3 and interested representatives from the MSCs. Once approved, a tentative UAV schedule is drafted and coordinated with the ACE for inclusion in the ATO.

ACE aerial collection requirements will be validated by the MAGTF G-2/G-3 and forwarded to the ACE COC. The ACE G-2/S-2 in coordination with the ACE G-2/S-3 will develop a collection plan that best uses available assets to collect the desired information. Requirements determined to be best satisfied by the UAV will be passed to the VMU for detailed planning in close coordination with ACE operations. Resulting UAV missions will be built into the ATO by the ACE S-3 and approved by the ACE commander. Requirements for operational support, such as assistance in adjusting supporting arms fire, go through the operations sections of MSCs and on to the MAGTF G-3/S-3.

Immediate

Immediate UAV missions are missions that were not previously anticipated or arise due to rapidly changing situations. Requests for support are submitted via the fastest means to the supported headquarters COC or FSCC. The urgency of immediate UAV requests must be balanced against the loss or postponement of preplanned UAV missions. The MAGTF commander will pre-define his collection priorities and re-tasking guidance. When an immediate request for aerial reconnaissance is submitted, the DASC/TACC will evaluate the request against available assets, current ATO tasking, and current MAGTF priorities and guid-ance. If the immediate request is of lower priority, the MAGTF COC will be notified and may or may not direct the ACE to re-task based on the current situation. Immediate missions can be executed in two ways:

- A dedicated UAV currently performing a mission can be diverted by higher authority to a higher priority mission.
- The MAGTF commander can order a standby UAV be ready for launch. When called for, this UAV is launched and the control station refines the mission plan while the UAV is out-bound to the objective area.

Note: If an immediate mission requirement arises while the UAV launch site is cold or not in a preflight/standby status, more time will be needed to prepare for launch.

Dynamic Re-Tasking

It may be necessary to alter the UAV mission as published in the ATO. The change may require a new route to fly to a new mission area, new altitudes or a new target for the UAV to exploit. Re-tasking that changes the preplanned route of flight must be coordinated with the appropriate air control authority (most likely the DASC) and the TACC. The DASC will ensure that all other airborne assets are adequately separated from the new route using procedural control measures. The TACC will ensure that air defense and intelligence agencies are notified of the change.

Nonorganic Assets

To obtain nonorganic UAV support, the MAGTF commander submits a JTAR to the joint force commander (JFC) J-2 for prioritization. The joint force air component commander (JFACC) determines the capabilities/sorties to provide the requested coverage and considers the request as part of the daily apportionment recommendation. Conflicting requests for theater-level UAV support are resolved by the JFC through the J-2's Daily Air Reconnaissance Board or similar forum.

Preplanned

A UAV liaison officer may be attached to the JFACC to provide technical and planning support. Once planning is complete, the fragmentary order and UAV schedule are submitted to the JFACC for inclusion into the ATO. The supporting UAV unit receives its mission via the ATO.

Immediate

The execution cell in the combat operations division of the joint air operations center normally develops immediate tasking. Immediate tasking supplements the ATO and modifies UAV tasking to support changing mission objectives. Tasking may include time-sensitive changes to the ATO, dynamic re-tasking of an airborne UAV or a new UAV mission. UAVs supporting theater-level operations may stay airborne for an entire ATO cycle, so it is common for such re-tasking to occur.

Flight Brief

The mission commander organizes a flight brief that includes the flight crew, intelligence representative, and maintenance representative. Briefs provide specific information in accordance with the VMU's SOPs. Briefers provide information to the entire crew to include the following:

- Weather update.
- Intelligence brief.
- System update.
- Mission profile.

Takeoff Methods

The maintenance crew readies the UAV for launch as the flight crew performs system checks to ensure systems perform in accordance with NATOPS procedures.

A vertical takeoff and landing require no length of runway for takeoff. However, a flat, smooth, clear area must be available for a safe, obstruction-free launch area.

If a suitable runway is available, the mission commander may perform a conventional rolling takeoff. The length of runway depends on the UAV. However, a 400-pound UAV requires at least 2,000 feet by 75 feet of hard, smooth, obstruction-free surface (at both ends of the runway) to allow the UAV space to climb to its pattern altitude.

If a suitable runway is not available, then the pneumatic launch method may be used. A launcher (part of the UAV system) drags the UAV along two rails and catapults the UAV into the air. It allows the VMU commander to accept an operating site that is unsuitable for conventional takeoffs, but can be used for conventional rolling recovery. Adequate surface area must be available for a safe landing for the UAV and clearance of nearby personnel.

If the RATO method is chosen, maintenance crews attach a RATO bottle to the UAV's undercarriage as it sits on a launch stand. The crew fires the rocket, propelling the UAV into the air. Like the pneumatic launch, adequate surface area for a safe recovery is required. The VMU commanding officer receives input from the UAV's pilot and mission commanders when determining the suitability of a UAV operation site and decides the most suitable launch method at that time.

Flight Crew

The mission commander is responsible for the overall conduct of the mission. He oversees and approves mission planning to comply with the ATO, flight schedule, and detachment SOPs. He forms and conducts the mission brief. UAV units may conduct split operations when the mission commander is not collocated with the UAV operator who launches and recovers the vehicle.

The internal pilot is responsible for the safe control and operation of all assigned UAVs as directed by the mission commander. The pilot may be involved in mission planning per squadron SOPs; completes all pre-launch, mission, and recovery checklists; and assists in evaluating and disseminating in-flight data.

The payload operator is responsible for the efficient and effective use of the airborne sensor. He operates the sensor; processes the data to be sent to command, control, communications, computers, and intelligence users; and recommends approaches and tactics to employ sensors.

The imagery analyst obtains, annotates, stores, and disseminates imagery or real time intelligence. He provides information for analysis and forming intelligence summaries to the intelligence officer. He also forms imagery reports as required.

The maintenance officer will ensure the payload is installed and pre-flight checks have been performed before staging and fueling to meet the flight schedule. The maintenance officer or qualified technician is available to the mission commander during the mission to assist with any system difficulties.

Dissemination

The VMU has an organic intelligence department that detects and interprets targets. The UAV video is linked to the G-2/S-2 section where intelligence specialists select, analyze, and distribute UAV imagery. Imagery can be digital photographs or splices of UAV video. With proper communications connectivity and bandwidth, these products can be posted on a Secret Internet Protocol Router

Network (SIPRNET) Web site and accessed by anyone with Web site access.

A copy of the entire UAV video can be created and delivered to the requesting unit. With proper communications connectivity and bandwidth, live video from the UAV can be provided over the SIPRNET. A live video product can be received by personnel within range of the remote antenna.

Preparing for Recovery

Upon return to the UAV operations site, flight and maintenance crews prepare for UAV recovery.

The mission commander obtains clearance to land from the appropriate air control agency, passes that information to the flight crew, and ensures the UAV recovery checklist is adhered to in accordance with the NATOPS manual. After recovery, the mission commander informs the appropriate control agency and the TACC that the UAV is no longer airborne.

The internal pilot monitors the UAV system and performs recovery procedures in accordance with the NATOPS manual.

The payload operator prepares the payload for landing and assists the internal pilot as necessary.

If the UAV requires an external pilot for recovery, control is passed to that position. Recovery procedures are conducted in accordance with the NATOPS manual.

Appendix A
Federal Aviation Administration
Regional Addresses

Federal Aviation Administration Alaska Region Headquarters ATTN: AAL-500 222 West 7th Avenue, #14 Anchorage, AK 99513	Federal Aviation Administration Central Region Headquarters ATTN: ACE-500 601 East 12th Street Federal Building Kansas City, MO 64106
Federal Aviation Administration Southern Region Headquarters ATTN: ASO-500 1701 Columbia Avenue College Park, GA 30337	Federal Aviation Administration Southwest Region Headquarters ATTN: ASW-500 2601 Meacham Boulevard Fort Worth, TX 76137-4298
Federal Aviation Administration Western-Pacific Region Headquarters ATTN: AWP-500 P.O. Box 92007, WPC Los Angeles, CA 90009	Federal Aviation Administration New England Region Headquarters ATTN: ANE-500 12 New England Executive Park Burlington, MA 01803
Federal Aviation Administration Great Lakes Region Headquarters ATTN: AGL-500 O'Hare Lake Office Center 2300 East Devon Avenue Des Plaines, IL 60018	Federal Aviation Administration Eastern Region Headquarters ATTN: AEA-500 JFK International Airport Fitzgerald Federal Building Jamaica, NY 11430
Federal Aviation Administration Northwest Mountain Region Headquarters ATTN: ANM-500 1601 Lind Avenue, SW Renton, WA 98055	

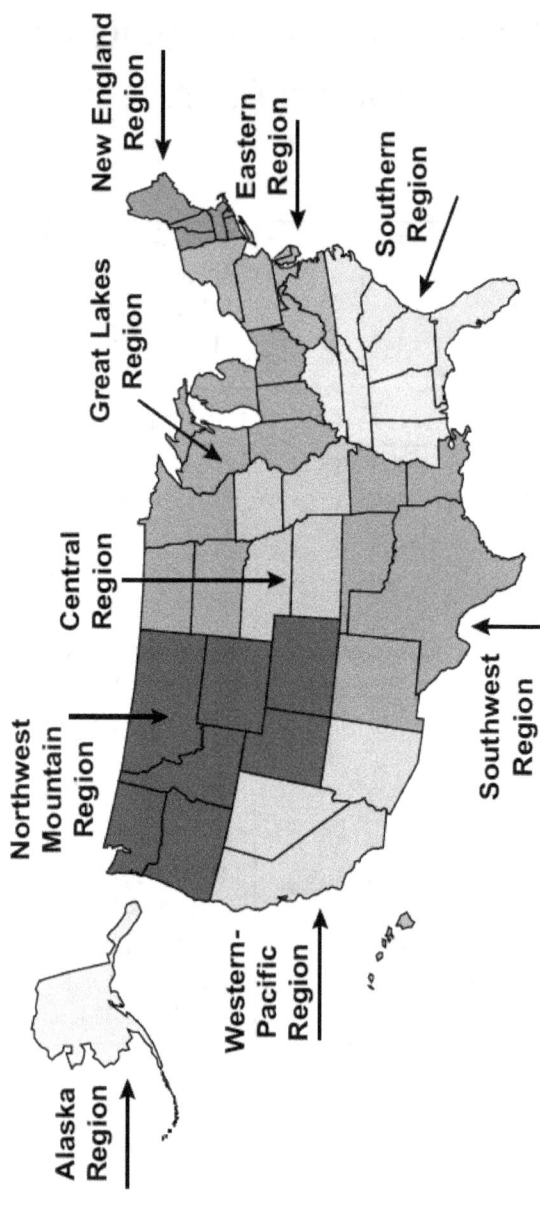

Appendix B
The Pioneer Unmanned Aerial
Vehicle System

General

The Pioneer UAV system consists of five Uavs, a ground control station (GCS), a tracking and control unit, a portable manually control station (PCS), and four remote receive stations. The UAV is manually controlled by a pilot from a control station or is programmed to fly independently under control of its autopilot. It is a fixed, high-wing aircraft used for RSTA operations, fire support adjustment, and bomb hit assessment. Driven by a pusher propeller, the UAV transmits video and/or telemetry information to the GCS and/or PCS in real-time. More than one control station may be used to increase the UAV's effective range or to control more than one UAV. The GCS is contained in an S-250 or S-280 shelter. When installed aboard ship, the GCS is contained in a mobile maintenance facility (MMF). The PCS does not require a shelter, and can be stored in an S-250 shelter.

Crew Requirements

The GCS in the S-250 shelter configuration or the MMF when aboard ship is manned by a mission commander, an internal pilot, and a payload operator. The GCS in the S-280 shelter is manned the same but also has an intelligence analyst to operate the intelligence bay. In either configuration, an external pilot is required during takeoff and recovery.

Principal Dimensions	
Wingspan	16.9 feet
Length	4.0 feet
Height	3.3 feet
Performance	
Service ceiling	12,000 feet
Maximum altitude	15,000 feet
Maximum endurance	5 hours
Maximum range	185 kilometers
Engine	26 horsepower
Fuel	AVGAS (100 Octane)
Cruise speed	65 knots
Maximum speed	110 knots
Weights	
UAV (empty)	276 pounds/l25 kilograms
Payload (maximum)	75 pounds/34 kilograms
Fuel	67 pounds/30 kilograms
Maximum takeoff	452 pounds/205 kilograms
Launch and Recovery	
Rolling takeoff (minutes)	210 meters
Pneumatic launch	21 meters
RATO	0 meters
Arrested recovery	130 meters
Shipboard Net Recovery	
Maximum headwind	25 knots, gust 30 knots
Maximum crosswind	15 knots, gust 20 knots
Maximum tailwind	5 knots (all launch types)
Weather	
Maximum winds aloft are at 60 knots. Flight in known icing conditions, instrument meteorological conditions, and precipitation is prohibited.	

Appendix C. Joint Tactical Air Strike Request (DD Form 1972)

JOINT TACTICAL AIR STRIKE REQUEST	See Joint Pub 3-09.3 for preparation instructions.

SECTION I - MISSION REQUEST

1. UNIT CALLED	THIS IS	REQUEST NUMBER	DATE		
				SENT	
			TIME	BY	

2.	PREPLANNED:	A PRECEDENCE _____	B PRIORITY _____		RECEIVED	
	IMMEDIATE:	C PRIORITY _____			TIME	BY

3. TARGET IS/NUMBER OF

A PERS IN OPEN _____	B PERS DUG IN _____	C WPNS/MG/RR/AT _____	D MORTARS, ARTY _____
E AAA ADA _____	F RKTS MISSILE _____	G ARMOR _____	H VEHICLES _____
I BLDGS _____	J BRIDGES _____	K PILLBOX, BUNKERS _____	L SUPPLIES, EQUIP _____
M CENTER (CP, COM) _____	N AREA _____	O ROUTE _____	P MOVING N E S W _____
O REMARKS			

4. TARGET LOCATION IS · CHECKED

A ____	B ____	C ____	D ____	BY
(COORDINATES)	(COORDINATES)	(COORDINATES)	(COORDINATES)	
E TGT ELEV ____	F SHEET NO. ____	G SERIES ____	H CHART NO. ____	

5. TARGET TIME/DATE

A ASAP	B NLT	C AT	D TO

6. DESIRED ORD/RESULTS · A ORDNANCE _____

B DESTROY	C NEUTRALIZE ____	D HARASS/INTERDICT

7. FINAL CONTROL

A FAC/RABFAC	B CALL SIGN _____	C FREQ _____
D CONT PT		

8. REMARKS

1. IP
2. HDNG _____ MAG OFFSET: L/R
3. DISTANCE _____
4. TGT ELEVATION _____ FEET MSL
5. TGT DESCRIPTION _____
6. TGT LOCATION _____
7. MARK TYPE _____ CODE _____
8. FRIENDLIES _____

9. EGRESS

THE FOLLOWING MAY BE INCLUDED IN THE "REMARKS", IF REQUIRED.

BCN-TGT _____ MAG BCN GRID ____ /
BCN-TGT _____ METERS TGT GRID ____ /
BCN ELEVATION _____ FEET MSL

SECTION II - COORDINATION

9. NSFS	10. ARTY	11. AIO/G-2/G-3

12. REQUEST	13. BY	14. REASON FOR DISAPPROVAL
APPROVED		
DISAPPROVED		

15. RESTRICTIVE FIRE/AIR PLAN		16. IS IN EFFECT	
A IS NOT IN EFFECT	B NUMBER _____	A (FROM TIME) _____	B (TO TIME) _____

17. LOCATION		18. WIDTH (METERS)	19. ALTITUDE/VERTEX	
A ____	B ____		A ____	B ____
(FROM COORDINATES)	(TO COORDINATES)		(MAXIMUM/VERTEX)	(MINIMUM)

SECTION III - MISSION DATA

20. MISSION NUMBER	21. CALL SIGN	22. NO. AND TYPE AIRCRAFT	23. ORDNANCE
24. EST/ACT TAKEOFF	25. EST TOT	26. CONT PT (COORDS)	27. INITIAL CONTACT
28. FAC/FAC(A)/TAC(A) CALL SIGN/ FREQ	29. AIRSPACE COORDINATION AREA	30. TGT DESCRIPTION	*31. TGT COORD/ELEV

32. BATTLE DAMAGE ASSESSMENT (BDA) REPORT (USMTF INFLTREP)

LINE 1/CALL SIGN _____	LINE 4/LOCATION _____
LINE 2/MSN NUMBER _____	LINE 5/TOT _____
LINE 3/REQ NUMBER _____	LINE 6/RESULTS _____
	REMARKS _____ · *TRANSMIT AS APPROPRIATE

DD FORM 1972, APR 2003	PREVIOUS EDITION MAY BE USED.	Reset

Appendix D
Glossary

Section I. Acronyms and Abbreviations

AAA ....antiaircraft artillery
ACA ....airspace coordination area
ACE.. aviation combat element
AO.. area of operations
AOA ....amphibious objective area
ATO ....air tasking order

BDA .... bomb damage assessment

CISP .... collection integration and synchronization
board
COC ....combat operations center
COF .... conduct of fire
CONUS ....continental United States

DASC ....direct air support center
DS ....direct support

EA .... electronic attack
EMW ....expeditionary maneuver warfare
EW ....electronic warfare
EWO...electronic warfare other

FAA ....Federal Aviation Administration
FSC........................... fire support coordination/coordinator
FSCC .... fire support coordination center

G-2 ....manpower or personnel officer (major subordinate commands and larger organizations)

G-3 ....operations officer (major subordinate commands and larger organizations)

G-4 ....logistics officer (major subordinate commands and larger organizations)

GCE ....ground combat element

GCS ....ground combat station

GS ....general support

HD .... helicopter direction

HF .... high frequency

HN ....host nation

IADS...integrated air defense system

JFACC ....joint force air component commander

JFC...joint force commander

JTAR ....joint tactical air strike request

LF .... landing force

MACCS ....Marine air command and control system

MAGTF .... Marine air-ground task force

MEF...Marine Expeditionary Force

MEU .... Marine Expeditionary Unit

MMF..mobile maintenance facility

MSC ....major subordinate command

NATOPS .... Naval Air Training and Operating Procedures Standardization

NGF .... naval gunfire

NSFS ....naval surface fire support

PCS..portable control station
POL ....petroleum, oils, lubricants

RATO .... rocket assisted takeoff
ROA ....restricted operations area
ROZ... restricted operations zone
RPV...remotely piloted vehicle
RSTA........................ reconnaissance, surveillance, and target
acquisition

SARC ....surveillance and reconnaissance center
SATCOM ....satellite communications
SIGINT..signals intelligence
SOP ....standing operating procedures
SPIRNET .... Secret Internet Protocol Router Network
SWO...senior watch officer

TAC .... tactical
TACC ....tactical air control center (Navy);
tactical air command center (Marine Corps)
TACT... tactical aviation control team
TAD...tactical air direction
T/E...table of equipment

UAV..unmanned aerial vehicle
UHF... ultrahigh frequency

VHF ....very high frequency
VMU ....Marine unmanned aerial vehicle squadron

Section II. Definitions

air control—The authority to effect the maneuver of aircraft. The elements of air control are: air control agency, air controller, airspace control, operational control, positive control, procedural control, radar control, and terminal control. Air control is the authority to direct the physical maneuver of aircraft in flight or to direct an aircraft or SAW unit to engage a specific target. (MCWP 3-25)

air control agency—An organization possessing the capability to exercise air control. (MCWP 3-25)

air defense—All defensive measures designed to destroy attacking enemy aircraft or missiles in the Earth's envelope of atmosphere, or to nullify or reduce the effectiveness of such attack. (JP 1-02)

air direction—The guidance and supervision which a commander employs to focus his resources on mission accomplishment. Air direction occurs as a sequence of the following activities: apportionment, allocation, tasking, and fragmentary order. The authority to regulate the employment of air resources (aircraft and SAW units) to maintain a balance between their availability and the priorities assigned for their usage. (MCWP 3-25)

air reconnaissance—The acquisition of information by employing visual observation and/or sensors in air vehicles. (JP 1-02)

airspace control authority—The commander designated to assume overall responsibility for the operation of the airspace control system in the airspace control area. Also called **ACA**. (JP 1-02) airspace control order—An order implementing the airspace control plan that provides the details of the approved requests for airspace control measures. It is published either as part of the air tasking order or as a separate document. Also called **ACO**. (JP 3-52)

airspace control plan—The document approved by the joint force commander that provides specific planning guidance and procedures for the airspace control system for the joint force area of responsibility and/or joint operations area. Also called **ACP**. (JP 3-52)

airspace coordination area—A three-dimensional block of airspace in a target area, established by the appropriate ground commander, in which friendly aircraft are reasonably safe from friendly surface fires. Also called **ACA**. (JP 1-02)

amphibious objective area—A geographical area (delineated for command and control purposes in the order initiating the amphibious operation) within which is located the objective(s) to be secured by the amphibious force. This area must be of sufficient size to ensure accomplishment of the amphibious force's mission and must provide sufficient area for conducting necessary sea, air, and land operations. Also called **AOA**. (JP 1-02)

area of responsibility—The geographical area associated with a combatant command within which a combatant commander has authority to plan and conduct operations. Also called **AOR**. (JP 1-02)

close air support—Air action by fixed- and rotary-wing aircraft against hostile targets that are in close proximity to friendly forces and that require detailed integration of each air mission with the fire and movement of those forces. Also called **CAS.** (JP 1-02)

combat information center—The agency in a ship or aircraft manned and equipped to collect, display, evaluate, and dissemi-nate tactical information for the use of the embarked flag officer, commanding officer, and certain control agencies. Certain con-trol, assistance and coordination functions may be delegated by command to the combat information center. Also called **CIC.** (JP 1-02)

combat operations center—The primary operational agency required to control the tactical operations of a command that employs ground and aviation combat, combat support, and com-bat service support elements or portions thereof. The combat operations center continually monitors, records, and supervises operations in the name of the commander and includes the neces-sary personnel and communications to do the same. Also called **COC.** (MCWP 3-25)

combatant command (command authority)—Nontransferable command authority established by title 10 ("Armed Forces"), United States Code, section 164, exercised only by commanders of unified or specified combatant commands unless otherwise directed by the President or the Secretary of Defense. Combatant command (command authority) cannot be delegated and is the authority of a combatant commander to perform those functions of command over assigned forces involving organizing and employing commands and forces, assigning tasks, designating objectives, and giving authoritative direction over all aspects of military operations, joint training, and logistics necessary to accomplish the missions assigned to the command. Combatant command (command authority) should be exercised through the commanders of subordinate organizations. Normally this authority is exercised through subordinate joint force commanders and Service and/or functional component commanders. Combatant command (command authority) provides full authority to organize and employ commands and forces as the combatant commander considers necessary to accomplish assigned missions. Operational control is inherent in combatant command (command authority). Also called **COCOM.** (JP 1-02)

combatant commander—A commander-in-chief of one of the unified or specified combatant commands established by the President. (JP 1-02)

combined arms—The full integration of arms in such a way that in order to counteract one, the enemy must make himself vulnerable to another. (MCDP 1) The tactics, techniques, and procedures employed by a force to integrate firepower and mobility to produce a desired effect upon the enemy. (MCWP 3-25)

command—The authority that a commander in the Armed Forces lawfully exercises over subordinates by virtue of rank or assignment: Command includes the authority and responsibility for effectively using available resources and for planning the employment of, organizing, directing, coordinating, and controlling military forces for the accomplishment of assigned missions. It also includes responsibility for health, welfare, morale, and discipline of assigned personnel. (JP 1-02)

command and control—The exercise of authority and direction by a properly designated commander over assigned and attached forces in the accomplishment of the mission. Command and control functions are performed through an arrangement of personnel, equipment, communications, facilities, and procedures employed by a commander in planning, directing, coordinating, and controlling forces, and operations in the accomplishment of the mission. Also called **C2**. (JP 1-02)

control—Authority that may be less than full command exercised by a commander over part of the activities of subordinate or other organizations. (JP 1-02) (Part 1 of a 4-part definition.)

control of aircraft and missiles—The coordinated employment of facilities, equipment, communications, procedures, and personnel which allows the ACE commander to plan, direct, and control the efforts of the ACE to support the accomplishment of the MAGTF's mission. (MCWP 3-25)

coordinating altitude—A procedural airspace control method to separate fixed- and rotary-wing aircraft by determining an altitude below which fixed-wing aircraft will normally not fly and above which rotary-wing aircraft normally will not fly. The coordinating altitude is normally specified in the airspace control plan and may include a buffer zone for small altitude deviations (JP 3-52). Used with US Army helicopters.

coordination—The action necessary to ensure adequately integrated relationships between separate organizations located in the same area. Coordination may include such matters as fire support, emergency defense measures, area intelligence, and other situations in which coordination is considered necessary. (MCWP 3-25)

deep air support—Air action against enemy targets at such a distance from friendly forces that detailed integration of each mission with fire and movement of friendly forces is not required. Deep air support missions are flown on either side of the fire support coordination line; the lack of a requirement for close coordination with the fire and movement of friendly forces is the qualifying factor. Also called **DAS**. (MCWP 3-25)

direct air support center—The principal air control agency of the US Marine air command and control system responsible for the direction and control of air operations directly supporting the ground combat element. It processes and coordinates requests for immediate air support and coordinates air missions requiring integration with ground forces and other supporting arms. It normally collocates with the senior fire support coordination center within the ground combat element and is subordinate to the tactical air command center. Also called **DASC**. (JP 1-02)

electronic warfare—Any military action involving the use of electromagnetic and directed energy to control the electromagnetic spectrum or to attack the enemy. Also called **EW**. The three major subdivisions within electronic warfare are: electronic attack, electronic protection, and electronic warfare support. a. electronic attack. That division of electronic warfare involving the use of electromagnetic energy, directed energy, or antiradiation weapons to attack personnel, facilities, or equipment with the intent of degrading, neutralizing, or destroying enemy combat capability and is considered a form of fires. Also called **EA**. EA includes: 1) actions taken to prevent or reduce an enemy's effective use of the electromagnetic spectrum, such as jamming and electromagnetic deception, and 2) employment of weapons that use either electromagnetic or directed energy as their primary destructive mechanism (lasers, radio frequency weapons, particle beams). b. electronic protection. That division of electronic warfare involving passive and active means taken to protect personnel, facilities, and equipment from any effects of friendly or enemy employment of electronic warfare that degrade, nuetralize or destory friendly combat capability. Also called **EP**. c. electronic warfare support. That division of electronic warfare involving actions tasked by, or under direct control of, an operational commander to search for, intercept, identify, and locate or localize sources of intentional and unintentional radiated electromagnetic energy for the purpose of immediate threat recognition, targeting, planning and conduct of future operations. Thus, electronic warfare support provides information required for decisions involving electronic warfare operations and other tactical actions such as threat avoidance, targeting, and homing. Also called **ES.** Electronic warfare support data can be used to produce signals intelligence, provide targeting for electronic or destructive attack, and produce measurement and signature intelligence. (JP 1-02)

emission control—The selective and controlled use of electromagnetic, acoustic, or other emitters to optimize command and control capabilities while minimizing, for operations security: a. detection by enemy sensors; b. mutual interference among friendly systems; and/or c. enemy interference with the ability to execute a military deception plan. Also called **EMCON.** (JP 1-02)

essential elements of friendly information—Key questions likely to be asked by adversary officials and intelligence systems about specific friendly intentions, capabilities, and activities, so they can obtain answers critical to their operational effectiveness. Also call **EEFI.** (JP 1-02)

fire support coordination center—A single location in which are centralized communications facilities and personnel incident to the coordination of all forms of fire support. Also called **FSCC.** (JP 1-02)

fire support coordination line—A fire support coordinating measure that is established and adjusted by appropriate land or amphibious force commanders within their boundaries in consultation with superior, subordinate, supporting, and affected commanders. Fire support coordination lines (FSCLs) facilitate the expeditious attack of surface targets of opportunity beyond the coordinating measure. An FSCL does not divide an area of operations by defining a boundary between close and deep operations or a zone for close air support. The FSCL applies to all fires of air, land, and sea-based weapons systems using any type of ammunition. Forces attacking targets beyond an FSCL must inform all affected commanders in sufficient time to allow necessary reaction to avoid fratricide. Supporting elements attacking targets beyond the FSCL must ensure that the attack will not produce adverse attacks on, or to the rear of, the line. Short of an FSCL, all air-to-ground and surface-to-surface attack operations are controlled by the appropriate land or amphibious force commander. The FSCL should follow well-defined terrain features. Coordination of attacks beyond the FSCL is especially critical to commanders of air, land, and special operations forces. In exceptional circumstances, the inability to conduct this coordination will not prelude the attack of targets beyond the FSCL. However, failure to do so may increase the risk of fratricide and could waste limited resources. Also called **FSCL.** (JP 1-02)

forward air controller—An officer (aviator/ pilot) member of the tactical air control party who, from a forward ground or airborne position, controls aircraft in close air support of ground troops. Also called **FAC.** (JP 1-02)

forward operating base—An airfield used to support tactical operations without establishing full support facilities. The base may be used for an extended time period. Support by a main operating base will be required to provide backup support for a forward operating base. Also called **FOB.** (MCWP 3-25)

ground alert—That status in which aircraft on the ground/deck are fully serviced and armed, with combat crews in readiness to take off within a specified short period of time (usually 15 minutes) after receipt of a mission order. Also known as **strip alert**. (JP 1-02)

identification—The process of determining the friendly or hostile character of an unknown detected contact. (JP 1-02)

identification, friend or foe—A device that emits a signal positively identifying it as a friendly. Also called **IFF**. (JP 1-02)

joint operation—An operation carried on by a force which is composed of significant elements of the Army, Navy or the Marine Corps, and the Air Force, or two or more of these Services operating under a single commander authorized to exercise unified command or operational control over joint forces. **Note:** A Navy/ Marine Corps operation is not a joint operation. (MCWP 3-25)

low level transit route—A temporary corridor of defined dimensions established in the forward area to minimize the risk to friendly aircraft from friendly air defenses or surface forces. Also called **LLTR**. (JP 1-02)

main battle area—That portion of the battlefield in which the decisive battle is fought to defeat the enemy. For any particular command, the main battle area extends rearward from the forward edge of the battle area to the rear boundary of the command's subordinate units. (JP 1-02)

maneuver warfare—A warfighting philosophy that seeks to shatter the enemy's cohesion through a variety of rapid, focused, and unexpected actions which create a turbulent and rapidly deteriorating situation with which the enemy cannot cope. (MCRP 5-12C)

Marine air command and control system—A system that provides the aviation combat element commander with the means to command, coordinate, and control all air operations with other Services. It is composed of command and control agencies with communications-electronics equipment that incorporates a capability from manual through semiautomatic control. Also called **MACCS.** (JP 1-02)

minimum risk route—A temporary corridor of defined dimensions recommended for use by high-speed, fixed-wing aircraft that presents the minimum known hazards to low-flying aircraft transiting the combat zone. Also called **MRR.** (JP 3-52)

naval surface fire support—Fire provided by Navy surface gun and missile systems in support of a unit or units tasked with achieving the commander's objectives. Also called **NSFS.** (JP 1-02)

near real time—Pertaining to the timeliness of data or information which has been delayed by the time required for electronic communication and automatic data processing. This implies that there are no significant delays. Also called **NRT.** (JP 1-02)

positive control—A method of airspace control that relies on positive identification, tracking, and direction of aircraft within an airspace, conducted with electronic means by an agency having the authority and responsibility therein. (JP 1-02) Also the tactical control of aircraft by a designated control unit, whereby the aircraft receives orders affecting its movements which immediately transfer responsibility for the safe navigation of the aircraft to the unit issuing such orders. (MCWP 3-25)

procedural control—A method of airspace control that relies on a combination of previously agreed and promulgated orders and procedures. (JP 1-02)

restricted operations area—Airspace of defined dimensions, designated by the airspace control authority, in response to specific operational situations/requirements within which the operation of one or more airspace users is restricted. Also called **ROA.** Also called **restricted operations zone (ROZ).** (JP 1-02)

rules of engagement—Directives issued by competent military authority that delineate the circumstances and limitations under which United States forces will initiate and/or continue combat engagement with other forces encountered. Also called **ROE.** (JP 1-02)

supporting arms coordination center—A single location on board an amphibious command ship in which all communication facilities incident to the coordination of fire support of the artillery, air, and naval gunfire are centralized. This is the naval counterpart to the fire support coordination center utilized by the landing force. Also called **SACC.** (JP 1-02)

suppression of enemy air defenses—That activity which neutralizes, destroys, or temporarily degrades surface-based enemy air defenses by destructive and/or disruptive means. Also called **SEAD.** (JP 1-02)

surface-to-air guided missile—A surface-launched guided missile for use against air targets. Also called **SAM.** (JP 1-02)

tactical air command center—The principal US Marine Corps air command and control agency from which air operations and air defense warning functions are directed. It is the senior agency of the US Marine air command and control system which serves as the operational command post of the aviation combat element commander. It provides the facility from which the aviation combat element commander and his battle staff plan, supervise, coordinate, and execute all current and future air operations in support of the Marine Air-Ground Task Force. The tactical air command center can provide integration, coordination and direction of joint and combined air operations. Also called **Marine TACC**. (MCWP 3-25)

tactical air control center—The principal air operations installation (ship-based) from which all aircraft and air warning functions of tactical air operations are controlled. (JP 1-02) US Navy only, US Air Force changed their TACC to AOC (air operations center).

tactical air operations center—The principal air control agency of the US Marine air command and control system responsible for airspace control and management. It provides real-time surveillance, direction, positive control and navigational assistance for friendly aircraft. It performs real-time direction and control, of all antiair warfare operations, to include manned interceptors and surface-to-air weapons. It is subordinate to the tactical air command center. Also called **TAOC**. (JP 1-02.)

target acquisition—The detection, identification, and location of a target in sufficient detail to permit the effective employment of weapons. (JP 1-02)

unmanned aerial vehicle—A powered, aerial vehicle that does not carry a human operator, uses aerodynamic forces to provide vehicle lift, can fly autonomously or be piloted remotely, can be expendable or recoverable, and can carry a lethal or nonlethal payload. Ballistic or semiballistic vehicles, cruise missiles, and artillery projectiles are not considered unmanned aerial vehicles. Also called **UAV.** (JP 1-02)

Appendix E
References

Joint Publication (JP)

3-09.3   Joint Tactics, Techniques, and Procedures for Close
Air Support

Marine Corps Warfighting Publications (MCWPs)

3-25   Control of Aircraft and Missiles
3-40.3   Communications and Information Systems

Miscellaneous

Unmanned Aerial Vehicle Survivability Threat Assessment Report,
Short Range Pioneer RPV System Survivability and Vulnerability

Pacific Missile Test Center and Joint System Threat Assessment
Report, Close Range Unmanned Aerial Vehicle (CR-UAV) (S)

NATOPS Operations Manual

DD Form 1972, Joint Tactical Air Strike Request (JTAR)